where do you go alone

pavana reddy

where do you go alone

Design by Adam Peña
Drawings by Mia Ohki

Printed in the United States of America
ISBN–13: 9781790237265
ISBN–10: 1790237262

For more information, or to order copies in bulk please visit pavanareddy.com

Front cover: Image of Kesarbai Kerkar's great grandniece, Shalaka Kerkar.
Rendition of an original photograph taken by Madhumita Nandi for *Untold
Collective*, 2015.

Back cover: *Pale blue dot*, captured by Voyager 1. Courtesy of NASA.

Title page: The first image of both the Earth and the Moon in a single frame,
captured by Voyager 1. Courtesy of NASA.

Author photo by Cristina Mirzakhanian.

"Jaat kahan ho, akeli gori, jaane na paiyyon"
Where are you going all alone, fair maiden, do your feet not know?

—Kesarbai Kerkar

Look again at that dot. That's here. That's home. That's us. On it everyone you love, everyone you know, everyone you ever heard of, every human being who ever was, lived out their lives. The aggregate of our joy and suffering, thousands of confident religions, ideologies, and economic doctrines, every hunter and forager, every hero and coward, every creator and destroyer of civilization, every king and peasant, every young couple in love, every mother and father, hopeful child, inventor and explorer, every teacher of morals, every corrupt politician, every "superstar," every "supreme leader," every saint and sinner in the history of our species lived there – on a mote of dust suspended in a sunbeam.

- Carl Sagan, "Pale Blue Dot"

In 1977, Voyager I was sent into interstellar space on a mission to reach a star 17.6 light-years from Earth. Included on the spacecraft was the Golden Record, or planet Earth's musical "message in a bottle", consisting of sounds and images selected to represent the life and diversity of our planet. The music chosen to be on this interstellar mixtape was handpicked by Carl Sagan and includes the likes of Guan Pinghu, Louis Armstrong, and Blind Willie Johnson. When I first listened to this record, one particular song which stood out for me among the rest was written by a singer from a remote hilly village in the heart of Goa known as Kesarbai Kerkar – a woman whose legacy on Earth has literally "crumbled to dust", while her voice still lives on far away among the stars.

Kesarbai's raga, "Jaat kahan ho, akeli gori" was launched into space the same year she died.

A billion years from now, when the Earth is nothing but dust, her voice
will serve as a reminder among the debris:

The universe wastes nothing.
What is lost is never truly gone, it is taken back.
What we create now will live beyond our own years.
This grief is only temporary.

Divided into five chapters named after the different full moons, this
book is meant to represent the cycles within each one of us.

Given the chance to do it all again, relive all the love, grief, joy and
heartache of being alive—would you take it?

Eventually, we will all be embedded among the stars.

This is my "message in a bottle" to the universe.

— pavana reddy

after a while
it doesn't matter who
leaves first,
we are becoming
what we always were.

before her very first
breath of dawn,
the moon said to the
newborn earth:

when you open your eyes
this will all become
temporary.

and the earth replied
by gazing directly
into the sun.

to my readers,

those who have found their way
and to those who are still searching,
thank you for visiting me where I go alone.

WOLF MOON

I wrote you into a poem,
the only part of me you have never visited.

I named every street after you.

a home is just a home
until you lose someone in it.

then it becomes a body.

I've buried your memory,
this body is a tombstone.

sometimes people visit me
they bring me flowers
they never stay.

everyone has a past.

each one of us carries
cemeteries beneath our skin.

your memory comes floating
back to me like wind through
a grave, like something long
buried trying to come back to life.

pain breeds wolves
and joys give rise to moons

we grow forests in our bones
so our memories can't find us

I believe we hide and haunt ourselves.

imagine all the lives you've touched
without even knowing it.

now think of all the strangers
who have touched yours
and tell me this world isn't
made entirely out of ghosts.

I have an entire forest
living inside of me
and you have carved
your initials
into every tree.

only you could
take up so much space
inside my heart
and still leave it so empty.

we fear ghosts
and yet we can't stop
making them out of each other
and praying they'll visit.

I've left many times before this.

but this,
this is different.

there is no escaping
someone who lives inside you.

there is no leaving.
there is no going home.

sometimes,
I go months
without remembering you.

some storms are like that.

I don't wish for your love anymore,
I have moved on and found my own.
but every now and then my mind wanders
and I wonder where I could have gone to.

are they your dreams I've slipped into
naked and full of moonlight?

do you wake up with the lingering taste
of my memory on your lips?

I'm sorry about that,

my thoughts have a habit of
running away from me
and you're usually the first place they go to
when they can't find their way back.

desire is a dark alleyway
and I am always taking
the wrong way home.

longing:

how soft a word
for such a ravenous feeling.

how we hunger in silence.

because I cannot touch
the tenderness of your throat
I squeeze the flesh of these words.

this poem is a strangled moan.

we swallow
our most tender secrets.

we love like carnivores,

by the neck.

tonight I am missing your hands the way a torn book misses its pages.

your memory kills me.

everywhere your skin has been
I have washed myself new,
scrubbed clean with the skin
of others.

I say that I've forgotten you,
that my bones are no longer
made of soil,
that your memory isn't
a vine snaking its way
around my throat.

I told you I didn't
need you to survive,
and I was right.

you call,
and I can't help
but hang myself
on your every word.

idle hands
do the devil's work
and mine are writing him love songs.

last night I wrote
a poem on your
back as the moon
ran her gentle fingers
through your hair.

did you feel it?

did the words crawl
beneath your skin
and darken your eyes?

I was hoping you could
wear them for me, the
next time your loneliness
walks you to my front door.

I'm so hungry for words
and you know how much
I love to watch you undress.

I want to be your chronic hungover
second mass confession.

I want to be the sin
your rehearsed parched tongue
swears to never commit again.

sometimes
when I miss you
I turn off the lights,
I let my thoughts
rest on your voice
until I can no longer see.

my hands tell me,
there's a language
to absence
only the skin knows.

I think I'm addicted to yours.

I know you.
I know you the way ash remembers burning.

you came into my life and suddenly
every dead charred thing inside me
sprung to life and whispered,
again.

if poetry
is simply
translating the heart
into words,
here's a poem for you:

I bleed
I bleed
I bleed.

I am still alive.

every seven years the cells in your entire body
will be destroyed and replaced with new cells.

I've been told that one day,
I will have a body you've never touched before.

this would be comforting if your touch ended with my skin.
if you never held my name like a religion
and pronounced my body like its prayer.
have you ever stepped inside an abandoned church before?
I tell people I'm getting better,
that I don't think about you that often,
that my cells are no longer pews filled with ghosts
when the truth is
I am like a home that has never known god
until it tasted loss for the first time.

we say time heals,
scab slowly spreading over wound,
that in seven years I will have forgotten you entirely.

I think whoever believes this has never really been touched.

you are the marrow of my bones,
graveyard buried beneath the church.

seven years can pass.
fourteen. twenty-one.
and I swear the mere thought of you
will still be powerful enough
to bring every cell of mine
to its goddamn knees.

I have you memorized by heart.

your absence
has become so real,
you've turned everyone else
into ghosts.

to think of love now is to imagine
a stem without petals,
of leaves that die in the fall,
for we were never meant to last.

I was so hungry for warmth
I fell for your touch
like winter starved of spring.

so tired,
I stripped the layers covering my heart
knowing I'd never be warm again.

we lose layers of
ourselves in others.

this is how we shed.

if only loneliness was a
place we visit and not
something we carry
around with us.

some people heal by loving you.
some people heal by breaking you.

you are my most tender wound.

how I ache
to be the memory
you fall asleep with.

some goodbyes never end.

they just linger,
like regret.

I will ignore these
billboards hanging
inside of me, this empty
city where every corner
is a comma, followed by
an ellipsis...I will ignore
the graffiti written on the
walls, the quiet chapters
we took with us to bed only
to abandon in the mornings.
I will ignore you smoothing out
the poems folded into the sheets,
the heaviness of the door closing
behind you, the reminder that I'm
a book you've read one hundred times
before, one-hundred-and-one.

sometimes, I can't find my way
home inside my own body.

this time when you left,
I renamed all the streets.

BLACK MOON

must the moon be full
in order to be loved?

and what of the heart?

little by little
I am forgetting you.

bit by bit,
I am disappearing.

each month I watch the moon
slowly erase herself.

I ask her,
why do you spend so much time
filling yourself
if you're only going to start all over?

she tells me,

to empty.
to forget.

I think of you
and I understand.

I finger your memories
like prayer beads
and watch as each of them
crumbles into dust.

the more I remember of you,
the less I become.

for fear of being alone,
we drank each other in
knowing how much
it would hurt in the morning.

the lies you tell yourself
to help you sleep at night
won't stick around for coffee.

I spend nights
filling your absence with stars
but when the morning arrives,
it is always just as empty.

be wary of whose world
you fall in love with.

the sky becomes a terrifying place
when you can no longer
lose yourself among its stars.

careful not to create books
out of people who only make room
for you to be a chapter of their own.

one day you will meet someone
who glows with a light that sets fire
to your heart and if you are lucky,
you will spend the rest of your life
next to them, warmed by a light
that can never die.

I pray when you find this person
they never leave.

the sad truth is,

some of us spend the rest of our lives
warmed by a fire lit by someone
who only stuck around
to share a spark.

the day you left
instead of following,
I told the universe
it was in her hands now.

I wouldn't beg.
I wouldn't go searching for you.

if it was meant to be,
you'd come back.

you never did.

I haven't forgiven her since.

this isn't a poem.

this is 4 am
wondering where you went
and why I was
too afraid to follow.

there are
some feelings
you will never
find words for.
you will learn
to name them
after the ones
who gave them
to you.

I wish I could love you backwards
so I could know what it feels like
to fall out of love with you
the way you so carelessly
did with me.

you touch as if you've spent
your whole life leaving

with you,
my body is a map
of all the places
you could never call home.

people aren't books I've learned.
you can't bookmark your favorite pages
to return to whenever you're feeling lonely.

when the nights get too cold
and you need something familiar to keep you warm,

you can't reopen their spines
wear out their pages
and call that obsession love.

I trust you
the way the shore
trusts the sea
to always leave
with part of her.

it's one thing to leave behind a bookmark
but to bend the corner
of someone's heart entirely,
that's a whole different kind of leaving.

that's the kind of love
that never intended to stay
to begin with.

don't talk to me about tomorrows.

there have been no new days
since you left.

only todays.

only minutes
seconds
moments
soaked in your absence.

most days I wish I never met you
so I could stop finding pieces of you
in the tangles you left behind.

in my hair. these words.
in this bed.

I am a poem in progress,
a tangle of words in search of some meaning.

some days I wake up
wondering where your
next poem will come from

I turn over to your side of the bed,
 a crumpled piece of paper,
and remember –

without you
every morning is a poem

and there is nothing
beautiful about it.

the longest distance
is between two people
who loved each other once.

it hurts right here,
in this very moment
seeing you smile
as if we never happened.
sometimes feelings can
take up the whole sky,
sometimes we don't notice them
until it begins to rain.
your face across from mine,
your laughter in the sunlight
growing daisies between
your teeth.

what was I to you,
other than the rain
watering your happiness,
the road you took
to where you are now?

I was the flowers in the
parts of the concrete
you loved to visit,
and now we no longer speak.

there is no poetry in loving someone
who is in love with someone else.

there are no words to describe
the pain in knowing I am like the dirt
giving shelter to your roots,
while you are the tree
dancing freely with the wind.

I told you I'd love you forever,
and I did.

it was you who cut forever
in half.

the hardest part
about losing a love
is having this new language
and nobody to speak it with.

who was I before
I learned your name?

what language did I speak?

we are afraid
to talk about
what hurts
because talking
requires breath
and there are
certain memories
we'd rather suffocate.

perhaps this is
the reason we write.

because sometimes,
words breathe better
than we can.

people just don't
have enough space in them
to be as forgiving as paper.

they run out so quickly.

I wanted to write you poetry
to show you how much I loved you

I wanted to share words,
but words have been used up
so tirelessly

so instead I've gathered
all of love's language
inside of my heart
so that I may be able to talk to you
the way lovers ought to,

in silence.

I used to love
being alone
until my alone
became you.

now even my
quiet screams
your name.

I am finding quieter ways to love you.

the poem
begins with so much
and always ends with you.

how is it that my love was too much for you
when I can't even find enough to give myself.

how dangerous love is.
how quietly it moves in
and rearranges
everything we know.

perhaps this is love's
true meaning–

an understanding
that two people hold the power
to rebuild each other's worlds,
and the trust in them never leaving
without putting everything
back where it belongs.

time meant nothing
when we were together.
I only spent a minute
next to you and somehow
a lifetime snuck past us
without a word.

how weightless the heart feels
carrying another's.

how heavily it falls
when the other lets it go.

the stars that fell in the night
gather on tulips and slowly turn to frost.

your absence is everywhere,
beautifully written
into the pale petals
I once planted for warmth.

if I cannot
have your love
I will take your rain.

pain has a heart.
be careful
not to confuse it
with your own.

the leaves of our days together
are slowly turning
and I am beginning to let go

but this cold in my touch,
this strain in my vision,
this new way in which
I speak,

when does that all
begin to fade?

there are days I wake up
and can no longer remember
who you are.

I think I dreamed you
into existence.

I often wonder
if I ever cross your mind
around the same time
you're crossing mine
and if we just keep
missing each other
on our way out.

I wonder farthest when I think of you.

I'm searching for a word
to describe that overwhelming
feeling of thirst in the midst of an
ever expanding ocean,
but all I can think of is you.

I've named many bodies
of water in your name,
and they have all drowned me
just the same.

I said not a word about you
but they saw the splashing in my eyes

they asked me if I needed saving
as if I was the one drowning,

as if I wasn't the sea.

so many broken hearts
living in pieces
pretending to be whole.

we cheat on each other
with memories.

we may sleep together
but it's our past
we take with us to bed.

time is a series of bookmarks we leave behind to visit by moonlight,
our past is the bedside book we reach for when we can't sleep.
we are melancholic by nature.

nostalgia wears you
like a perfume.

I smell you everywhere.

perhaps we will meet again
as characters in a different story.

maybe we'll share a lifetime then.

BLOOD MOON

I still touch myself
when I think of you,
like I'm covered in blood
but I can't find a wound.

a man calls me darling
and I turn into a dark forest,
a secret hidden beneath the flowers.

I smile a hungry smile.

how dangerous it is
to be a woman
defined by a man.

a soft woman
is simply a wolf
caught in meditation.

he said,
you're so full of yourself.

I replied,
I am.
I am.

and I'm not sorry
if that threatens you.

if he doesn't love you
the way you need to be loved
for god's sake leave.

life is too short
to keep breaking your back
for someone who refuses to grow
a spine of their own.

there is strength in love
so darling grab her by the hand
and walk away,
don't bother looking back.

he won't stop you.

the spineless ones never do.

you are not a graveyard.
stop opening your heart
to those who are only looking
for a place to rest their tired bones.

he said,

a girl made from splinters
isn't ready for love.

I told him he was wrong,
it's men like you who
are afraid.

men with gasoline hearts
and ravenous hands.

men who crave the fire
but don't know how
to handle the flame.

when you said you loved me and left anyway,
you taught me I was beautiful
in all the wrong places.
so I took a candle and painstakingly
searched my entire body for everything ugly
and found only words.

I had to set myself ablaze
to see that I am beautiful
in my entirety.

I am an unfinished poem
spreading like wildfire,
and that's why you left –

I was beginning to grow,
and you were too afraid
of getting burned.

sometimes you have to learn how to be the ash before you can become the flame.

teach him never to claim
where he has still yet to learn.
men will chart and map our bodies
as if we haven't lived there
our entire lives.

when he leaves,
make sure you know
your way back to yourself.

I hope you remembered to keep a light on.

and before you ever let someone new inside,
remind your heart:

if you must fall in love with a stranger,
let it first be with yourself.

I'm not telling you to leave him,
I'm telling you that when he reaches
for the glistening gold of your skin,
make sure he recognizes the sharpness of the blade
from which you shine.

I'm not saying you deserve better,
but when he compliments the earth of your body,
I hope he can name everyone you once were.

every woman it took to nourish you.

I think about
all the women
I used to be.

I am a different ghost everyday.

you cannot have
my heart and wash
yourself of its blood
at the same time.

today I am
waking all the
women
I once was.
I am washing
the dirt
from their hair,
I am kissing
the flowers
from their eyes.
today I am
greeting myselves
with forgiveness
and letting
them go
at the same
time.

my mother always said,
girls are like water.
don't let the rock hearts
of men take that away from you.

I'd ask her,
but doesn't water smooth stone?
why is it okay for them to be rough
and our job to soften?

she would then envelop
my small hands in hers,
a soft ocean swallowing a river.

she'd say,
rocks smoothed by water
are still rocks, they forget.
they can still crush you.

it's water that remembers.
water both softens and drowns,
water is the quiet river
before it is the raging sea.

you were not made
to soothe the hearts of men,
you were made to become the ocean.

even if that means drowning a few along the way.

water is never silent.
even the quietest river
holds a deeper,
more complicated meaning.

my heart is so much like the sea.
when it rains,
she grows.

the ocean is fluent in every language
and still chooses to speak with meaning.

she tells me,

never pay attention to
those who speak ill of you.
you were not born half sea
so you could listen to the
chattering of tiny rivers.

you were born to swallow them.

remember this, girl.
you are half sea.

no one ever asks
the ocean to quiet her storm,
so why do you keep
apologizing for yours?

an ocean of a woman
is worth the storm.

you feel like winter,
my mother says.

cold. what is this?
I did not give birth
to you beneath the sun,
name you after spring
so a man could change
your weather.

so what if he left.
how dare you dim
the light I gave you
for someone who
only wanted to take it away.

love lost is a gift.
why wish for its return.
why beg for its flame
when you've already been burned?

is it not enough to live
from day to day remembering
its tune like a beautiful melody
you heard years ago?

is it not enough
to see a bruise
and remember how it blossomed?

love is a song we hear
only a few moments in our lifetime
but it's that memory that is the gift,
the way we remember is what lasts forever.

stop ruining love by wanting what no longer exists.

your soul is beaming with flowers.
it's time to stop watering your scars.

deserving better doesn't always mean
being with someone.

sometimes it means gathering everything
they took for granted and bringing it
back home to yourself.

let them go.
your heart has been full
for so long now,
it's time to let it breathe.

a woman smiling
is like the sun,
she doesn't shine for you.

what should you look for
in a man?

the woman in him.

search for her.

I am a word.

at worst,
a poem.

at best,
a revolution.

I'm not impressed by the kind of beauty
which requires eyes to see.

we live in a society that treats
girls like flowers, the prettiest
recognized at their youngest,
picked to satisfy selfish desires.

what a curse it is to be a flower,
to be chosen for beauty only to
die in the hands of an admirer
before she can fully bloom.

you tell a girl
she's beautiful
enough times,
eventually she'll grow
to believe it.

now imagine
what would happen
if you named her brilliant.

I promise
you've never seen
a star shine so bright.

the only thing more detrimental
than society's unreal expectations
on how a woman should look
are the abiding women who
perpetuate these stereotypes.

how can we set fire to the very thing
built to destroy us if we can't stop
scorning the ones wielding the flame?

Her Name Meant Dream

for women of color
whose bodies are made of clay,
we are a world map of loss.
when they ask me where I'm from
I no longer name a country, but you.

dear sister,
when they ask me for your name
I hesitate out of fear of you drowning in their ignorance.
I've already lost you once.
instead, I give them your meaning:
I come from a dream,
from a tune I'm desperately trying to remember the words to,
that I haven't been able to sleep right since.

dear sister,
I am sorry for turning you into a poem,
it was the only way they'd listen.
the world doesn't have patience for stories about brown girls
convinced their life isn't worth living.

I'm sorry the only time they call you beautiful
is when you're neatly pressed against their white space –
so relatable and unthreatening in your pain.

I am sorry, because there was nothing beautiful about your death.

for women made of clay,
fire and water have paved our bodies burning and softening our souls
into molds of our ancestors, shapes out of our dreams.

I want to tell you that I grew up to be half the girl you wanted me to be
and in a way, I did. I grew up to be a writer,
and you, you are the color of my ink.
everything I write is stained with you.

but even with you next to me
there are days I wish I could erase everything.
days when I still have to justify my skin to more people
who look like us than the ones who killed you.

days when I can't stop seeing tears silently fall
off mom's face as she reassures her mother back home that she is happy;
days when I have to listen to my co-worker from Idaho tell me,
we are all immigrants.

an ocean of words foam in my mouth
that I want to spit back at her,
demand what she had to sacrifice to be here,
but the immigrant in me makes me bite back.
keeps me silent. makes me swallow my own blood.

I'm tired of reminding people
that no one just happens to leave entire countries.
I'm tired of marching with women who need reminding.

dear sister,
the day you died mom asked me if she could rename me after you,
I told her she didn't have to.

if I never had a home before
I do now in these words with you,
that even though I am so tired
I will continue to hold your name close
and cherish it the way dreams ought to be cherished.
I will fulfill you the way the world never could.

dear sister,
if only you could see how your words have helped
so many young girls who look like you.

it's a dream come true. I just wish you were here to believe it.

·   ·   ·

surviving you is a slow death.
storm clouds swallowing the bluest sky.
you see the rain coming, but you've
learned to stop running.

surviving you is being named
brave for something I did not
earn nor want. It's listening to
strangers console me for my loss
when you were never lost, you
went away.

surviving you is reading about a
nine year old boy who learned the meaning
of suicide before tolerance, another
memory buried beneath bouquets
of hashtags grown from poisoned earth.

surviving you is watching a mother
bury her own child. it's what turns
people into seasons,
the most beautiful parts of them
always struggling to hold on.

surviving you is a reminder of all
the ways we die and bring ourselves
back to life; it is accepting that
your departure was less a suicide
than it was a form of self-preservation,
a reminder that this world still hasn't learned.

surviving you is why I am more graveyard than body.

more altar than flesh.

perhaps this is why I refuse to allow the earth
of my bones to claim me.

surviving you is the reason I am alive,
my body's way of remembering.

surviving you is a prayer:

I will take this grief.
if it fills me with you.

•   •   •

if we trace everything back far enough
we always return to nature.
in Houtouwan China, a ghost village is found
beneath a thick blanket of greenery.
what is left behind can also flourish.

in the end, we are all abandoned.

if a mother's womb is as far back as our minds can fathom,
what kind of scenery grows within her now?
I imagine the inside of her to be a haunting and beautiful place.

in Kerala, a Dalit mother finds the mutilated body of her daughter
stolen by men secretly attracted to the night.
everything comes back to where it began.
a mother's womb swallows her emptiness.
a daughter killed for her place in this world
is taken back by the earth to grow again.

in the end,
we are all new growth spreading over haunted towns.

we age,
not by years,
but by stories.

the time is coming.
one sweeping tide to wipe the shores clean.
a time that will bring back our land,
our languages, our voices, our poems.
hidden beneath centuries of lies.

a time that will open our souls
to ourselves, one giant flower
grown from burnt earth.

the ancestors, living and gone,
are rising to remind the world
that us women have always been
part of nature.

my sisters,
do not let go of that patience
you've been brewing your whole life,

for our season is approaching.

in a world full of Eve's
I stand with women
who wear serpents around their hips
and paradise between their legs.

you left and I met a new woman,
a woman hidden inside of me,
beautiful as the moon hidden
beneath the sea,
she rose into my night.

you left,
and I am no longer alone.

I guess that's why I fell in love,
so I could rise out of it.

your silence is a song. your silence is a love letter I will never read.
your silence is the sweetness of a sitar learning the language
of the rain and I am drenched in you.
your silence is a god I now believe in.

the urn of your throat where I've left my ashes.
your spine, a candle-lit memorial through a thick forest of veins.

I am lost in you.
I like to lay beneath the sky and think of you,
a mesh of constellations ending beneath my skin.
I think of the night of your flesh,
the coffin of your lashes closing over me,
the ebony of it.
the velvety sinking depth of it.

the night is an idol I am praying into flesh.
you are shiva dancing on a dying atheist's bed.
there's a reason why no one believes
until there's nothing left to believe in.
in my final steps down your star-lit spine I whisper,

I believe. I believe. I believe.

you deserve a love so big
it dims the sky and sets fire to the stars.

a love so expansive,
it weaves constellations
so you never forget who you are.

you wear silence like a skin
and I love lying naked in your arms.

listen carefully,
the strongest love
is a quiet love.

trust in your silence.
the universe hears you.

when does a thing you fear
stop being something you fear?

when you stop feeding it.

when you take it into your bed
and love it in the sunlight
as you do in the dark.

trust in the weight you carry.
no one knows
the strength of your bones
more intimately
than your spine.

our souls never met,
they hugged
as old friends do.

she led me to her
the way the waterfall
leads to the sea.

the way we fall
and blame it all on fate.

you were written
before you became a word

you have always been a poem.

I could learn how to speak
every language and still not know
how to say *I'm home* as meaningfully
as the sun stirs your skin awake each morning.

you asked me once if I believed in magic.
I said yes with you I feel warm,
our skin burning like forest fires
in each other's hands.

what I meant was,
my palms blush
when I think of you.

the sun herself is written
into our future.

I think I've known it
since the first time we touched.

it's been nothing
but light since we met,
she said.

I smiled.

I told the sun
about you once.
I think she poured
herself into me
so she could feel you too.

I love her,
I have tasted
the honey of her name

my chest is now a beehive
listen,

they call her queen.

meeting her was like writing a poem.

I had to sit with her for a while,
let my thoughts rest on her like raindrops
until they were ready to bloom.

writing has become a stroll
through a rain kissed meadow since.

I loved to watch her hands
while she spoke,
the way she felt words
before speaking them.

her touch left poetry
running down my skin,
as if her very fingers
were made from music.

please stay with me awhile,
you're a poem I've been
wanting to write my entire life.

your soul is so
beautifully written,

I've plagiarized you
in every poem.

———

more than the desire
to be loved
or heard
or seen,
I desire to be read.

to be understood
in one's own language
is an erotic thing.

did the word come before the poem
or did the poem come first?

each night I wonder
as our tongues discover
new parts of each other
to pronounce.

your mind does things to my body
that your hands never could

you touch me in places
I never knew existed.

she kissed me as if everything
she has ever been silent about
finally found its way to the surface.

she kissed me
and I drowned.

what else do you do with a love that deep?

when the ocean loves you,
what else can you do
but feed her your bones?

in this lifetime you will experience 3 types of love:

a love that will give you words

a love that will take them away

and a love
that will teach you
a whole new language.

I hope you grow to learn the difference.

I woke up in a poem,
still wrapped in their music
like someone's favorite journal.

and it finally feels good,
knowing that I will leave
this bed still smelling of you.

it's been so long since
I've been kissed as if
every curve of my body
were a syllable,

I'd forgotten what it felt like
to be held like a meaning
and not just a word.

I want to do
loud things
quietly
with you.

I love the way
you undress
when you think
no one is reading.

my body stutters around you.
my mind becomes a run-on sentence.

where does your light
come from, the one that
cuts so deep into my thoughts.

what darkness was it born from?

I am never alone.
my solitude
has her own moon.

while you were lowering your eyes
to take a sip of coffee, a train outside
was swallowed by a tunnel and for a second,
every passenger was engulfed in darkness.

at that moment, I started thinking about
all the things that could happen when we look away,
the universe we miss in the blink of an eye.

but then you set down your cup
just as the train disappeared into the distance
and lifted your eyes to meet mine,
and you smiled that smile
that always makes me forget the universe.

your love has passed
through me like a light
through a stained glass
window, now anyone I
allow inside falls in love
with your colors.

my lips are still
stained with you.
I haven't changed
colors since the
last time we
kissed.

I love you
because in a world
filled with nights,
you taste just like morning.

Tirupati

in Andhra Pradesh India lies the Tirumala Temple,
situated upon a hill where devotees of Venkateswara
flock from all over the world to climb. I used to pass
by the stairs leading up to this hill every day and watch
as the first rays of sunlight softly crept up all 3500 steps
as if on pilgrimage for some higher meaning. my grandma
used to tell me that I would miss this place once I leave,
that people come from all over the world to climb the
summit I pass by everyday, as if they all carried questions
tied to their backs and only the top held the answer.

I told her they were foolish for doing it.
she told me I was like the sun
that is raised in the east
only to settle in the west.

there's a way in which you wake up each morning,
as if the world hides inside the corners of your mouth
waiting for dawn to break.

you remind me of home –
of bent backs and softly folded hands,
of Sanskrit chants and hopeful hearts,
of believers and of those who no longer do.

I asked my grandma once,
what do all these people expect to find at the top?
she laughed and said,
they come out here to leave their questions behind.

now I know that you and I don't believe in gods as
much as we believe in the sky and everything she
holds, but the way the morning hides behind the
sleeping mountain of your body has me believe that
maybe we are all on a journey to answer the heaviness
tied upon our backs, and perhaps the journey is in
leaving it all behind.

I guess what I am really trying to say is, I think the
sun goes to sleep every night with a new question
tied to her back, and I think you have always been
the place she goes to find her answer.

॰   ॰   ॰

when the sun spreads herself
over your body,
I forget for a moment
that the world is round.

you were a puzzle piece
that didn't fit into my life
until I picked up a pen
and painted a whole new picture.

you are the reason my life has become
a work of art worth completing.

no one knows
what love is.

he says,

flowers stars
the moon

she says,

birth fire
light

before they came,
I swear the flowers
didn't even know
how to blossom

the stars were candles
lit by their hair,

even the moon orbiting
their naked limbs
forgot the meaning
of vastness.

I loved them with all my heart
and they loved the way I healed.

you don't need someone
who understands your pain
you need someone who can hold it.

we forget too often
that not everyone with a heart
broken in all the same ways
knows what to do with the pieces.

I am a hundred
different shapes
around everyone else,
but with you.

with you,
I am solid.

you know how a bird
held captive for too long
approaches an open cage slowly
as if unsure of their freedom?

life seems so full of those moments.

life is as short as the flutter of a wing
and I am filled with bluebirds.

you are a mystery to me
yet so familiar,
like a song I've never heard before
and a tune I've known my entire life.

this is how I knew:
you held my name
inside that language of yours,
you pronounced me
the way I've always dreamt
of being understood.

you cradled my name
inside your tongue
and whispered,
welcome home
as I sat in-between
your teeth thinking:

I know this language.
I think I've known it
far longer than I have known you.

we are like night and day.

we are two strangers
who have always
known one another.

I love you
because when I am with you
I never have to leave myself.

wait for someone whose kiss envelops you
like dawn stretching over the night sky.
have you ever seen the way night and day touch,
that brief moment in which two days melt
into each other before parting ways?
wait for that.
wait for someone who will possess you like night
and set you free like morning.

love once filled me
like a field of daisies
but hope stripped away
all of their petals.

I come to you now
as a naked stem
with nothing to offer
but the promise of growth.

can you love me truly?

for you,
I will blossom once more.

your love grew flowers out of the darkest parts of my heart.

tonight beneath the wildflowers
the moon is a silver apple dangling
from a naked branch

the night is the ink I write your name with

these stars are your words.

in the dark forest
of your mind,
take me where
the wildflowers grow.

HARVEST MOON

I am half a moon
where I once
held a heart.

I am not broken,

I am simply
on my way
back to myself.

even the moon
needs time
to remember
how fully she is loved.

on her very first
descent into the sea,
the sickle moon
said to the rising sun,

I am filled to the bones
with you
and yet still so hungry.

the sun smiled at her,
a full smile
that lit every dark crater of her heart.

that's what love is,
it's the power
to swallow you whole
and leave you full
at the same time.

and the moon,
in all of her phases,
never once forgot
the sun's words.

so he left and you grew lighter.
you expected this,
the danger of losing yourself
in someone else,
of having them leave
without giving you back.

in the mirror you still search your body
for any remnants of him,
each time your fingers come out dry.

you still call him your first love
as if he were a definition
and yet your heart lays scattered all over the floor.

you call him your first love
and yet you're the one broken
trying to pick up the pieces.

didn't anyone ever tell you?
your first love isn't the one
you gave your heart away to.
your first love is the one who
makes you forget everyone
else who threw it away.

so he left and you started to grow.
you never expected this to happen,
to grow roots from ashes,
you never expected to blossom.

so here you are now,
a tree stripped of its dead branches.
here you are now,
growing back into yourself.

no one ever told you
that your strongest parts
are everything they couldn't take with them.

no one ever told you
that your first home
and your first love
will always be you.

*   *   *

learn from the river,
the art of moving on
without ever letting go.

your heart does not
hold fortunes, no one
needs to break it
to know what you
hold inside.

one day you are going to learn
how to give all of you away
and still come home
to yourself.

the art of putting your heart
into something without
taking it out of yourself.

the happiest time in my life
was when I stopped caring about
whether or not you noticed.

this is the last poem of longing
sent shivering to the wind
for you no longer have a home inside of me.

may your cold memory find warmth
inside someone else's bones.

autumn is the poet of all seasons.

fallen leaves upon flaming earth,
the beauty in setting fire to the things
we can no longer hold onto.

she asked me how long it would take,
for this pain to go away.

there's something to writing,
the act of putting a pen to paper –
almost like performing surgery,

suddenly everyone expects you
to magically stitch some words together
to heal their wounds.

I told her it didn't work that way,
that when you throw a rock
through a window, it only shatters once.
the mess is in cleaning up all the tiny shards.

she laughed.
so you're telling me I'm too fragile?
like glass?

no, I reassured her.
I'm saying that even when you think
you've cleaned everything up,
you can still cut yourself on all the
tiny pieces you missed.

I'm telling you that sometimes
healing is the longest,
messiest thing you will
ever have to do for yourself,
but you're doing it.

you don't need a poem.

you're the most beautiful poem I know.

don't apologize for leaving.
for making room for me
to fill each gap with
more of myself.

for teaching my heart
how to beat harder
and warmer
on her own.

be kind to your pain,
be patient.
it is trying to understand
why you hurt.

the bitterness will set in once you learn
he found a home in another woman's body.
you will trace the craters of your own, blame
each imperfection for being the reason he
chose her instead. you will curse her name.
pray that he may never taste the fullness of
a kiss again, that she will always ever be just
a sliver of the moon you once were.

the night will creep in through your locked
windows, cold dark fingers reaching for the
softness of your throat because his memory is
still a tide living deep within you. days and days
like this will go by until one by one the women
in your life find you and let themselves inside.
this is what women do – we hear each other loudest
amidst silence. we untie the fingers from
around each other's necks, we teach the heart a
new prayer:

I no longer wish to be the woman you can't let
go but the woman you always remember. let my
memory no longer be a ghost but a slight breeze
through your heart whenever she is hurting.
when she can't remember her own name.
isn't ready to say I love you back.
remember me and love her harder.

this is no longer a wish that she may never
be the one but a prayer she becomes your
everything.

the truth is, every woman you meet is a
hidden full moon and for her sake I hope you
learn to love in a way that sets her light free.

even if that means forgetting.

even if you only remember me
as the kind of full moon
you will never witness
in this lifetime
again.

◦   ◦   ◦

I don't want to be the woman you can't stop comparing everyone after me to.

I want to be the woman who teaches you to stop comparing women.

keep all the pieces
of me you took
when you left.

I think you
needed them
more than I
ever did.

I love in drafts.

when I call a book my favorite I mean,
I read this during a time I needed it most.

I mean,
I've read many other
beautiful books since,
but this one will always hold
a special place inside my heart.

and when I said I loved you
what I meant was,

my heart is a bookshelf
and you will always be
one of my favorite stories.

if someday
the weight
of your heart
suddenly gets
too heavy,
think of me.

I've finally
stopped carrying it
inside my own.

you are the main
character of your own story
and the architect
of your own happiness.

everyone else is simply a visitor.

never trust your weakness.
it knows nothing about you.

I call it destiny
when you grow
from a place
someone left you in.

people are made out of space.
everyone you meet and fall in love with
creates a tiny world within you and when they leave,
that space fills with emptiness.
so you close the door to that world
do your best to never visit it again
refuse to let the light in,
allow that room you once loved so much to sit in darkness.

one day when you least expect it,
you'll let someone new inside.
before you know it
you've got a galaxy whirling inside you.
stars are forming.
doors you didn't even know were locked are opening.
light is flooding the floors.

you'll walk past that door you locked so long ago.
pause outside. crack it open expecting darkness
and you'll see nothing but stars.
you'll sit beneath them. marvel at their vastness
and how small you truly are.
you'll smile at their memory,
the home you built together,
pause before leaving but this time -
you leave the door wide open.

you go back to your budding galaxy,
and you love them the way
that tiny world could never love you.

if it's written
in the stars
it's written in
your scars.

you were made from
the dust of light,

within your wounds
lies a whole universe
just waiting to be born.

the universe is made of holes.
chasms. voids of nothingness.

you are empty space.
you are uncharted territory.
you are the slivers of sunlight
shimmering in-between matter.

your bones are fragile,
your veins transient.

that pain in your chest
between your heart and
your skin is a gap, a galaxy,
an ethereal space full of
endless possibilities.

science cannot explain
the stabbing sensation we feel
whenever our hearts break
the same way it can't
explain the universe,

but you are more than matter.

you are the spaces between words.
you are the moment before a second.
you are the entire universe held within a single body,
and this is why you feel.

you are empty,
but you are also full of galaxies

and this is why no one understands you.

around you floats the entire universe.
it's impossible not to feel alone sometimes.

we all have our space in this world.

stop searching for yours
inside someone else.

as is a star
so is a galaxy.

as is an atom
so are you.

we are born
uncharted like the stars

we spend our lives
weaving constellations.

the moon and the stars
are anchored to the night,
heavy like the darkness
within you.

but you mustn't let
the night crush you
darling,
just breathe.

for the sunrise
needs you
too.

you pray for good things
to happen to you,
but close the door on yourself.

you pray for happiness,
but you don't even know
how to let yourself inside.

read books
ride buses
take walks
speak to your loneliness.

the trees in the rain,
the way they bend and endure –
this is how some hearts learn to heal.

no one knows
the way to love
but we continue to move
in its direction.

we all start out as naked spools
slowly gathering threads of the past
and we leave this world just as empty.

we are not defined by what we hold onto,
but how beautifully we weave our lives
out of the threads we learn to let go.

when I fell in love
it was like looking into
the most unforgiving mirror
and seeing myself smile
at every hidden flaw.

no one else can heal you
the way you heal yourself.

that is your own special magic.

be your own magic
your own fantasy
your own spell.

prove your own myth
by cultivating yourself.

the way the river flows,
peaceful and serene
even in the midst
of a burning forest.

to continue flowing
in one's own direction
as if nothing ever harmed you.

you are not the dirt
you are planted in.

you are the light
and the water
you nourish yourself from.

you are the flower
you choose to be.

and so what if you don't belong?

a fish will only grow to fit within
the borders of its confinement,
but that doesn't make it small.

you were made for greater things.

you don't belong not because
you can't find a place in this world,
but because the world is too small
to fit the universe that is you.

if you are unhappy with your story
remind yourself that you do not
have to see it through.

a happy ending isn't always
in the way things turn out,
but rather how you choose
to end the things which bring you
unhappiness.

water doesn't simply become the sea,
it has to take on many different forms
before joining with the ocean.

just like the raindrop,
the stream,
and the river,

you are meant to become
many different people
on your journey to yourself.

your bones had to grow
to allow you to become
the person you are today,
there's no good reason
why your heart can't
do the same.

love. love until it kills you.
keep loving until the only
other choice you're left
with is to live again.

we are made of the sky
and of the sea.

the power to create the storm
and to bear
it is within us.

it's been said that the
faces we see in our dreams
are always faces we've seen in real life,
whether we remember them or not.

I think this is why so many of us
compare love to dreaming,
or a familiar melody wafting down the street –
you try hard to recognize it,
chase it around the corner,
but by then it's already too late.

I think this is what people mean
when they say *I fell in love.*

they mean,

we bumped into each other
while we were out
chasing something else.

these untold stories come in many forms:
a face in passing, an old book hidden
behind a bookshelf,
the fleeting memory of a dream.

they mean,

I've been waiting
my entire life
for someone to see me.

a love like ours
happens only once
a lifetime, and I have
chosen yours in every
one of them.

I think you're a poem
and everyone before you
has been a story,

you move in different
languages.

what's the word for,

your very heartbeat
has a thousand bluebirds
lined up at the window
in anticipation.

I'd love you to the moon
and only to the moon

I'd love you enough
to never go back.

hold language close to you, like a lover.
make love in verse.

your name on my tongue
was how I knew
destiny had a taste.

I loved you and discovered more of myself.
what a strange feeling, to meet someone
who owns every key to the parts of yourself
you didn't even know were closed.

this is what I know:

there's a forest growing
inside of me and each
leaf trembles with a song

you are the prettiest face
that has ever broken into
a smile for me

when our eyes meet,
I earthquake.

I'm convinced that all rivers
are silent eulogies carrying
our secrets to their graves

my veins are tiny rivers,
you are the sea.

I swear to always remember
your love the way the ocean
remembers the moon.

darling,
I am possessed by
your light,
your lips,
and every story
they hold in-between.

it's a race against dawn
to kiss you in all the places
the sun loves to call home.

the dream is not
in disappearing,
this I could do
on my own.

the dream
is in you
coming with me.

there are some oceans I have
never crossed whose salt
runs through my veins,

paths I have not yet followed
whose flowers blossom
within my heart,

feet I have never walked beside
whose footprints line my soul,

and there are some people
I have only just met
yet have known my entire life,
for we are of the same star.

when you touch me,
a moon rises.

you have always been my sunset.

I have to believe in the idea
of more than one soulmate,

how else could my soul
recognize you
if she hadn't always
known herself?

the moment our souls met,
I understood what it was to be blind.

your love must be the light
that first set fire to the stars.

you're unpronounceable to me,
like silence.

you're everywhere
and I still can't name you.

love,
it passes
but it does not die.

this life is simply
the birth of our love.

before us,
the universe
was our womb.

before us,
we belonged to the stars.

may the moon remember you in waves.
may you be written
into the petals
of a burning sun.

I will no longer shed tears
for anything that does not cause me to bloom.

FLOWER MOON

you stroll through my mind
and flowers blossom beneath your feet

loving you has always been
part of my nature.

I remember feeling your touch for the first time
so soft, it turned my bones into flowers.

people are like that
I've learned,
our hearts memorize them

some people take root inside
the marrow of our bones
and grow there.

you are the silence I turn to
when everything else gets too loud.

you are my moon in the middle of the day.

the moon is as ancient
as time itself
and still no older than a month.

I am trying to learn from her,

the art of growing
without ever losing my child within.

today I woke up thinking of you
and laughed anyway.

I stretch out on my bed
fill all the spaces I used to call yours
and let the sunlight kiss me good morning.
I eat breakfast
pack my lunch
go to work
with a smile on my face.
no one asks me why I'm so happy,
after all this me is no different
from any other me – those days when
I wake up with your memory hung
like a windchime around my tongue,
when I cannot speak without
my words bumping into you.

I've gotten so good at pretending,
sometimes even I begin to believe it.

my friends notice and ask if I'm doing better
and I don't have the strength
to tell them the truth,
that you've become the air inside of me.
some days you're the wind
most days you are the hurricane
but today,
today you are summer
blooming beneath my skin

that even on my warmest days,
I still breathe you.

things that break:

flowers
dawn
the ocean
our hearts

this is how
gardens grow

this is how
the sun blossoms

this is how we
make it home

this is how we
learn to love.

I was told
to fall in love
with my eyes
closed, but

my heart

is still
learning
the art of
opening up, she

blossoms

secretly
in the dark,
searching

for

ways to be
happy,
alone,
without

you

the poetry of being alive together,
of sharing a quiet space in the same sentence.

we've been fragments
of each other
our whole lives

we are a poem.

I am in love
with the depth
of your mind,
I could lay among
your flowers
hidden beneath
the grass
and fall asleep
for hours.

do you feel me
dreaming?

does the grass
take my form?

tell me,
do you ever notice me
loving you, at all?

falling in love with you
was like taking a delicious
afternoon nap.
I promised myself
only the briefest slumber
but as soon as I had fallen,
I was already dreaming.

my entire sky craves
only your star.

there's a rhythm you make
when I put you into words,
it's a tune I just can't get
out of my head.
each morning I rise
with a new song
blossoming on my lips.

you are like the tree
whose magnificence lies not only
in the strength of her branches,
but in all the birds who trust those branches
to build their homes.

a memory:

my mother braiding my hair beneath the lemon tree,
their fragrance relinquished into the air
as she hums a tune under her breath

today in my own garden,
the scent of lemons growing stronger
as I unbraid my mother's hair
each untied strand,
a release

the breeze visits us for a while,
she gathers a few lemons and disappears
with the rest of our song
singing softly,

there's a candle in you
that can never be undone.

honey runs through my skin.
I am a petal in the west,
a flower whose roots
carry the blood of the east.

my mother's arms grow strong
from tending to her garden.
hands cracked. shoulders bent. knees bruised.

night and day she tends to her rose buds,
her legs sore and her eyes wet
from caring for her loose leaves and
dying branches, how she cried when my roots
travelled too far from her loving care.

my mother's soul lives inside her garden
and her heart blooms with every petal
that unfolds,

fingernails split from digging soil
and planting seeds, how they used to
split from my dirty dishes and hand
washed laundry.

my mother's children live inside
her garden and how they love her
for the care she gives them –
so selfless and true.

and how she loves them all the more
for always needing her, too.

what growing up in this country
taught me:

weeds are often names
given to the flowers
we were taught to never pick.

your mind is the only country
you truly belong to

treat it that way

don't let anyone inside
who doesn't respect
the earth you're grown from.

the ability to find so much beauty
in a language who continues to deny
the existence of mine,
that is love.

person of color:

a strange fruit
plucked by hands
not of the land.

flesh torn and consumed,
seeds spit back into the earth.
buried whole,
told to never grow again.

those who rebelled
grew to no longer
recognize the earth.

give me a home that isn't my body,
a land where I am no longer a foreigner

give me a country that I don't belong to,
a place I can slip in and out of like a
vagabond free of roots

give me a body that I can visit
as a guest greeted with warmth

strip away this skin
where I am so much a stranger
trying desperately
to belong.

India and Pakistan:

we are two bookshelves
who have never touched
because of all the history
between us.

there is no justice
in a country
who continues to weep
with one eye closed.

Remain the Sea

mother swallows golden sand
whispers, she's taking back what's hers.
her feet are two split continents
her heart is the map of the world.

lay with me through my storm
she says, *be the moon to my sea.*

I ask her,
but where does the heart go
when it's taken from the motherland?

I'm like the sky, pregnant with life
and searching for a safe place
to empty.

mother crashes her body against the shore,
says *pain is what we carry upon our backs*
love is being silent about the weight.

the death of the motherland
is not in what we leave behind
but in everything we forget,

and you are not so privileged.

you are a child of fire and water.
the strength to be the storm
and to carry it is within you.

so storm, she says
and I will carry your every drop.

the body is a continent
but may your heart
always remain the sea.

we are drifting continents
we are broken land
we are the earth's mosaic,
the dust beneath generations of feet.

we have lost ourselves
trying to claim the sea,

we have forgotten
that in the end
it is the sea who claims
each one of us.

I'm not made from the kind of earth that buries.

I'm made from the kind that resurrects.

no one has ever hurt me
the way I've hurt myself

I've always been
a bouquet of blooming flowers

the only difference is,
I grew every one of them.

some days
I am the flower

some days,
I am the rain.

tend to the earth.
tend to her women.

perhaps the light
from the sun
isn't as selfless
as the poets love
to write about.

perhaps
we just haven't
been listening.

we must learn to bear pain
the way the earth bears her seeds,

we must learn to blossom from it.

I plant seeds when it rains.
I am always in bloom.

it isn't the pain you deserve,
it's the healing.
you're going through this
because you deserve to grow.

some days
it storms,
some days
it shines.

this is how
flo(we)rs
grow.

when it rains,
something new blossoms
in all the spaces
the sun could never reach.

when people leave
they leave behind a garden
and lately I've really been into
reopening old wounds and setting them aflame.

I read somewhere that some flowers
can only grow after the ground above them burns,
the same flame that destroys also gives life.

your leaving was a blessing I never expected
because it lit a slow fire within me
and it's with this fire I am learning to grow again.

thanks to you,
there is nothing left in me to burn

and thanks to me,
there is only room to grow.

I'm a flower
when it comes to love

I shed with intention.

learn me slowly,
please be patient
with my pages.

not emptiness

but space

the words we think
but do not speak
become the person
we try to hide from
the world.

I visited my past
to water their trees
and found nothing
but a barren field
echoing the sound
of bluebirds,
so I returned to today
carrying new seeds
to bury in my
own garden
and waited
for the bluebirds
to follow.

the love you deserve can unlock doors
but chooses not to.
doesn't break down walls,
doesn't turn into rain
and seep into the cracks
you forgot to close.

the love you deserve
won't force its way inside,
it's patient love,
waiting on the porch
with flowers in their hands.
knows you are worth the wait,
knows that they are overflowing with love,
knows that it still isn't enough
if you do not know
how to love yourself.

the love you deserve
sees you through the cracks
and marvels at your wholeness,
wonders how you could deny
yourself of yourself.

wonders how the moon would rise
if there was no ocean to welcome it.

thank you
for growing flowers in me
where I could only grow graves.

how beautiful it is
to have someone
who loves me for
more than the flower
I am, but for each
fading petal

I forgive in flowers,
I plant seeds where it hurts.
I take my time,
I blossom first.

I had to dig myself out of you,
this is what it means when you ask me
how I've been and I tell you
I've been blossoming.

and what do the flower buds
pushing up from the broken earth
say about you?

we break to grow.

love softly. love quietly.
love like the heart is a flower
and you are morning rain.

rain in my heart
dirt in my bones
flowers in my soul.

the sun can't seem
to let you go.
I rise thinking of you.

I sat down to write at seven,
determined to be finished with you at last.

I listened to the rain outside
as I thought of the right words
to end your story with,
but only silence filled the page.

I put my pen back down,
suddenly absorbed in thoughts
about the rain, when had it begun?

looking down at my journal
I flipped back to the beginning of our story,
a blank page shining secretly like
a wet cobblestone pathway
leading somewhere promising.

picking up my pen,
I followed.

do not grieve
for the sinking moon
when the skies
are on fire.

thankful for the moon
who never forgets to feed herself,
who teaches me how to stay full
even on my hungriest days.

thankful for the peace
that follows the storm,
thankful for my hurricanes.

thankful for the river,
how she always flows
in her own direction,
thankful for every bridge
I burned along my way.

thankful for the salt
inside my veins, the oceans
that have carried me away from home,
for the patient way the sun teaches me
how to drown and blossom again.

thankful for the soil,
for teaching my heart
how to grow a garden
out of the things we bury,
thankful for every flower.

thankful for this lotus life,
for its relentless bloom.
for wearing beauty like a shield,
despite the dirt
always
despite the pain.

one thousand times over
would I endure
the unbearable briefness of this life
for one eternal moment
with you.

Acknowledgments

28   Inspired by an original piece by Brett Elizabeth Jenkins, who wrote
the following poem to beautifully describe healing after trauma:

> It's said it takes seven years
> to grow completely new skin cells.
>
> To think, this year I will grow
> into a body you never will
> have touched.

132   In loving memory of Jamel Myles.
No child should learn the meaning of suicide before tolerance.

134   In loving memory of Jisha, and to every woman taught her voice does
not matter because of her place in this world.

291   *Remain the Sea* written for the album, *Land of Gold*,
by Anoushka Shankar

Thank you to everyone who was a part of this book's creation, both
knowingly and unknowingly.

Each one of you is a wildflower grown from the darkest parts of my heart.

The biggest thank you to my sister.
In my heart, we are still in Canada. It's snowing outside.
We are cuddled together on the staircase and I'm asking you
to read *The Call of the Wild* to me again for the hundredth time.
If you're annoyed, you never show it. Instead you smile and
open the book, and together we vanish to somewhere
only we ever go alone.

pavana reddy is a los angeles based poet and songwriter.
this is her second collection of poems.

With love,

Lavrana Reelely ♡

60311_9781790237265
06.01.2020 1529

With love,

Pavana
Reddy ♡